ELEANOR OF AQUITAINE

A Life From Beginning to End

Copyright © 2018 by Hourly History.

D0012576

Table of Contents

Introduction

Eleanor of Aquitaine began life in the shadows, as was typical for a medieval woman. It is only at the time of her father's death and her marriage to King Louis V of France that she begins to appear in the historical records. Even then, scholars infer much of her role and influence as queen of France from manuscripts of questionable veracity or from letters in which Eleanor is not directly mentioned.

From these beginnings, Eleanor rose to a position of great prestige and power. She was the wife of two of Europe's kings and the mother of two more. Not only did she have great influence over the lives of these men, but she also had opportunities to rule herself—in her own duchy of Aquitaine and her neighboring province of Poitou, as well as in England, where she governed in place of her husband or son during their absences. Beyond this, Eleanor is a tantalizing figure for historians because she was something of a rebel. She was likely a major figure in achieving the annulment of her first marriage, and she took an active role in working against her second husband, King Henry II of England, in favor of her sons—setting herself not only against her husband but also against the mighty medieval authority of the church.

Given Eleanor's wealth, reputation, and powerful position, along with the scattered nature of the sources that give us information about her life, it is perhaps not surprising that the many gaps in our knowledge about her life have been partially filled by legends, many of which have become popularly accepted as fact. Some of these legends arose during medieval times, not long after Eleanor's life, while others are the result of the conjectures of historians closer to our modern day. In this book, you will find an attempt to sort through these legends and distinguish the facts that are available to us from conjectures that have little basis to present a balanced telling of the story of Eleanor of Aquitaine, one of medieval Europe's most memorable women.

Chapter One

Duchess of Aquitaine, Queen of France

"I place both my daughters under the protection of my lord the King. I entrust [the older one] to him so that he may give her in marriage, if my barons consent, and bequeath to her Poitou and Aquitaine."

—Testament of Duke William X, *Ex Fragmenti Comitum Pictaviae*

Aquitaine—in the twelfth century, a duchy of great wealth and power—sits in south-central France. Duke William IX, born in 1071, cut quite a memorable figure as duke. He lived in frequent conflict with the power of the medieval church and engaged in behavior considered scandalous by his medieval society. He somehow escaped the wreck of the First Crusade, founded a monastery, suggested the creation of a convent made up of prostitutes, was nearly excommunicated (or perhaps actually was), and at last brought his mistress to live openly in a tower of his palace at Poitiers—while his wife Phillippa retreated to a life in the monastery he had founded. William's wild and sometimes contradictory life is most often remembered for his role as the first of the troubadours—medieval French poets who envisioned an ideal of courtly love, where a woman's love was envisioned to be an almost divine source of salvation and bliss, worthy of the patient work it took to court and win her affection.

Duke William IX was the grandfather of Eleanor of Aquitaine. Although, as a very young child at his death in 1126, Eleanor would hardly have known or remembered William IX, his life and his legacy undoubtedly had an influence on Aquitaine for many years to come—and, by extension, on his granddaughter. William IX's son, Duke William X, was Eleanor's father. William X, though lacking the flamboyant personality of his father, also had his share of conflict with the church. Reconciliation with the church may be the root of William X's decision, in 1137, to set off on a pilgrimage to Saint James of Compostela. In any case, this pilgrimage led to his death at Compostela.

It is at this point that William's daughter Eleanor appears in the narratives of history. Historians estimate the year of her birth as being either 1122 or 1124, making her 13 or 15 years old in 1137. William X had no male heir since his only son had died years before. Upon William's death, Eleanor, heir to the rich realm of Aquitaine, was left under the guardianship of the king of France, Louis VI. Louis's power as king of France was quite limited. Dukes of powerful holdings such as Aquitaine, Normandy, or Burgundy could operate largely independently of the king, despite his technical role as their overlord.

In fact, some of these dukes had not even shown up for Louis's coronation. The responsibility of arranging a marriage for the wealthy young Duchess Eleanor provided Louis VI with an advantageous opportunity—he would marry Eleanor to his son and heir, Louis VII. The conditions of Eleanor's inheritance stipulated that she would retain control of her holdings in Aquitaine, but the union would create a powerful alliance for the king of France.

Young Prince Louis, 16 years old at the time, had not expected to be heir to the throne of France. That role was supposed to belong to his older brother, Philip. Louis had been on his way toward a pious life within the church's cloisters when Philip died in a riding accident in 1129. Louis was almost immediately crowned as joint ruler with his father, but his early days of training for an ecclesiastical life would leave their mark on him.

By the time the young Louis was sent to Aquitaine by his father in the summer of 1137, everyone knew that King Louis VI's health was failing. He was known as "The Fat" and on top of his obesity was suffering from dysentery.

Prince Louis traveled through France with 500 knights. In Bordeaux's Cathedral of Saint Andre, on July 25, Louis of France married Eleanor of Aquitaine. As a wedding gift, Eleanor gave Louis a famous rock crystal vase that she had inherited from her grandfather William IX, who had received it as a gift from a Muslim ally—whom some scholars believe was the last king of Saragossa, in Spain. This vase now rests in the Louvre, the only physical relic of Eleanor's life that remains in modern times.

After their wedding, Louis and Eleanor journeyed toward Poitiers, capital of Aquitaine. There, they officially became duke and duchess of Aquitaine on August 8, 1137. Until that day, they were unaware that Louis VI had already died on August 1. Anticipating the potential upheaval that might accompany succession to the throne, Louis and Eleanor hurried toward Paris by way of Orleans. Eleanor, still only a girl of 13 or 15, began a new life in a new city—she was now not only duchess of Aquitaine, but also queen of France.

Chapter Two

Eleanor and Louis Joins the Crusade

"From the very first she had by her beauty so enslaved the young man's mind that, when he was preparing for that most famous expedition, he was so passionately in love with his young wife . . . that he decided to take her with him to the war."

—*William of Newburgh, Historia Rerum Anglicarum*

Despite being the queen, Eleanor was an outsider in Paris. Historians have long characterized Eleanor as high-spirited, a product of the bold, more secular culture of southern France—a sharp contrast to the more conservative and austere customs of northern France and Paris. Louis began to spend extravagantly—a move that seems out of character for the pious king but may have been an effort to please his new wife. Many scholars see these cultural differences at the center of the conflict that would soon erupt.

Additionally, while evidence is scarce, some historians also suspect Eleanor may have influenced a variety of Louis's political moves. In the year following Eleanor and Louis's wedding, 1138, Louis defeated a significant rebellion in Eleanor's holding of Poitiers with only 200 knights accompanied by archers and siege engines. In 1141, he began an expedition to claim Toulouse, which Eleanor should have had the rights to through her grandmother, Philippa. Perhaps Eleanor even had an impact on other changes that occurred around 1141, as the Abbot Suger—previously a trusted advisor—seemed to hold lessening influence in the political scene of France.

Before long, however, events took a turn that made Eleanor's influence more marked. Her younger sister, Petronilla, had become romantically involved with the king's cousin, the over 50-year-old Raoul de Vermandois. When the couple wanted to get married, Eleanor interceded for them with the king. King Louis lent his support to Petronilla and Raoul's marriage, despite one major obstacle that came with a huge risk—Raoul was already married. Raoul's wife was the niece of the powerful count of Champagne, Theobald. Crossing Count Theobald—not to mention the immense authority of the medieval church—to promote a marriage between Raoul and the young Petronilla (who was at the time about 15) could carry a real risk of war.

Nonetheless, Louis helped Raoul find clergymen who would allow him to escape his marriage, using consanguinity—too close of a kinship between a husband and wife—as the grounds. As a result, Raoul and Petronilla were married in 1142. Count Theobald, as expected, did not take this dismissal of his niece lightly. He appealed to the Pope, who, in conjunction with a council, determined that Raoul's annulment of his previous marriage was invalid. Raoul and Petronilla both faced excommunication.

King Louis, in response, raised an army and marched on Champagne. There, he attacked the capital, Vitry. His victorious army lit houses on fire in the city, and before long the church also burned. Over 1,500 of the city's people had taken refuge in the church, and they died in the fire. This was not the end of Louis's war in Champagne, though some records do claim that he vowed to go on a pilgrimage to Jerusalem in penitence for the deaths in Vitry. An attempt on the part of Abbot Bernard of Clairvaux to stop the war by asking the Pope to reverse Petronilla and Raoul's excommunication (without agreeing to their marriage) only resulted in Louis's statement of opposition to marriages planned for Count Theobald's children, and warfare in Champagne continued for two years.

In June 1144, Louis and Eleanor, along with Louis's mother, Adelaide, and many other nobles, traveled to the Abbey of Saint-Denis for the consecration of a new part of the church building there. Bernard of Clairvaux would also be at Saint-Denis. Knowing that Eleanor, along with all those from Aquitaine who supported her, was the primary instigator in the attempt to have Raoul and Petronilla's names cleared, Bernard took an unusual approach—he held a private meeting with Eleanor. He used her lack of children after seven years of marriage and resultant fear of infertility as a bargaining tool, telling her that if she ceased her rebelliousness toward the church and her negative influence over her husband, she would have a child.

In exchange for his prayers, Eleanor at last agreed, and peace was established. Louis and Count Theobald came to an agreement, with Louis stopping to lay waste to Champagne and Theobald calling off the marriages that Louis opposed. Louis also reconciled with the church, recognizing the Pope's choice of archbishop of Bourges, whom he had also previously opposed. Petronilla and Raoul remained excommunicated. Bernard's prediction for Eleanor, however, came true. In 1145, she gave birth to her first child, Marie.

Louis had begun making plans for a pilgrimage to Jerusalem—perhaps due to the burning of Vitry, though scholars suggest a variety of other possible motivations. Before long, news arrived that the key city of Edessa (present-day Sanliurfa in south-western Turkey) had fallen to the Turkic Zengid dynasty. With this report, the plans for pilgrimage quickly turned into plans for a crusade. During the Christmas of 1145, Louis announced that he would "take the cross"—the vow of the crusaders. In this decision, most of the church leaders, such as Bernard of Clairvaux, did not wholeheartedly support him. The idea of a king leading a crusade carried with it great danger and risk.

One of the main sources describing this event, though written 30 years later, tells of how Eleanor received the cross as well, becoming a crusader alongside her husband. Other historians credit Louis's love for Eleanor and refusal to leave her in France as the reason that she joined him on the crusade. Some modern scholars even note that Eleanor's uncle was reigning as Prince of Antioch, which, with the fall of Edessa, became more open to Muslim attack; they suggest that Eleanor was behind the idea of the crusade, motivated by aiding her uncle. Despite these and other varied speculations, there remains no actual evidence as to what Eleanor thought or wanted in relation to the crusade. Eleanor's presence did have the benefit, for Louis, of gaining him support from Aquitaine. Her barons contributed to Louis's military strength, and Aquitaine also helped support the campaign financially.

In February of 1146, Louis and his advisors met to plan their expedition. Several months later, Louis, his mother, and Eleanor returned to Saint-Denis, where Louis would meet with the Pope and with Abbot Suger. Suger was to be left in control of France—with the help of Raoul and the Archbishop of Reims—during Louis's absence. A monk from Saint-Denis, Odo, recorded how Louis, after venerating the relics and receiving the Pope's blessing, retreated from the crowds into the relief of the monks' cloister, leaving Eleanor and his mother outside.

After this, Louis and Eleanor began their journey. They traveled overland, first heading toward Constantinople, the heart of the Byzantine Empire. The huge company traveled slowly. Relations with the Byzantine representatives who came to meet the crusaders did not go well—the Byzantines looked down on the barbarian Westerners, while the crusaders saw the Byzantines as soft, deceitful, overly deferential, and hardly true Christians.

Odo, who chronicled the journey, mentions that among the many messages the Byzantine Emperor Manuel sent to Louis, there were also sometimes messages from the empress to Eleanor. A Greek writer who described the French crusaders wrote about how their women rode like men and carried weapons. He compared them to the mythical Amazons and likened Eleanor to the queen of the Amazons, Penthesilea. Many later writers and scholars, inspired by his depiction, began to build on the image of Eleanor and the women who traveled with her, elaborating on the idea of the women as Amazon-like warriors—one of the many unsubstantiated legends that have come to surround Eleanor's life.

As the crusaders approached Constantinople, conflict with the Byzantines escalated. The crusaders discovered that Emperor Manuel had signed an agreement with Turks—another sign of the Byzantines' untrustworthiness to King Louis and his followers. The crusaders stayed in Constantinople for three weeks. Some scholars have made a case for the idea that Eleanor was enamored with the luxury and splendor of the Eastern city and the Byzantine court—a world remarkably different and more thrilling than the life in the court of Paris.

The French crusaders' stay in the city ended when they received a report that Emperor Conrad of the German Holy Roman Empire had achieved a great victory over the Turks. Wanting to take part in the glory of routing the Turks, the crusaders headed east. Even their departure was not without conflict—a Flemish crusader stole money from a moneylender and was followed by other crusaders.

Ultimately, to settle the dispute, not only was the man hanged, but the Byzantine Emperor insisted that the French nobles pay him homage for any conquered territory.

As the French crusaders entered Anatolia, where Emperor Conrad had supposedly won his victory, they received a shock. The message had been erroneous—Conrad had not been victorious but had suffered a terrible defeat. Joining with the piteous and weakened remnant of the German forces, the French continued to march toward Antioch, where Eleanor's uncle ruled. Their route led across the Phrygian Mountains where disaster struck.

Louis commanded his vanguard to stop and camp at the top of the pass at Mount Cadmus. Louis's uncle, the count of Maurienne, and one of Eleanor's vassals, Geoffrey of Rancon, were in charge of the vanguard. Arriving early, they decided to continue into the valley rather than stopping. But by becoming so far separated from the rest of the company, they gave the Turks an ideal opportunity. The Turkish forces struck the middle part of the company, which contained baggage, carts, and many unarmed pilgrims. They then carried the attack on towards the rear guard, which King Louis commanded. Though the king himself escaped, many others died.

The blame for this tragedy (by Odo's account) was placed upon the count of Maurienne and Geoffrey of Rancon. Odo recorded that "all the people thought that Geoffrey ought to be hanged for disobeying the King's orders." However, it was clear that the blame belonged equally to the count of Maurienne, who was the king's uncle—and thus, according to Odo, "must obviously be spared." So neither one of the men was hung.

Despite the fact the neither Odo nor the later chronicler William of Tyre, who obtained his information second-hand, give any information about where Eleanor was during this attack, a legend has developed that she was with the vanguard and that the whole mistake was either partially or entirely her fault. She has been blamed for the massacre in various ways, from the idea that she ordered Geoffrey, her vassal, to head down to the valley, to the thought that she must have agreed to Geoffrey and the Count's plan, to the idea that the company had too much baggage and was slowed down primarily because of Eleanor and her women.

These ideas, like many of the other myths around the figure of Eleanor, are based on conjectures rather than evidence. It is possible that the accusations resulted from her association with Geoffrey, or simply because of her role on the crusade as a woman—a position that came under much criticism from those who wrote about the Second Crusade, such as William of Newburgh. Historian C. H. Walker concluded that this legend came about later when Eleanor was being used as a scapegoat for other issues.

From Mount Cadmus on, the company of French crusaders was often under attack. These attacks and the constant losses they entailed drove King Louis to turn to the sea—leaving most of his foot soldiers behind when he could not find or pay for enough ships. These soldiers met an unhappy end, facing deprivation and illness before finally falling prey to Turkish attacks. However, Louis, along with Eleanor and what remained of his cavalry and entourage, finally arrived in Antioch in March of 1148. In Antioch, the constant conflicts that had characterized the crusade would become more personal for Louis and Eleanor.

Chapter Three

The Royal Divorce

"When the King came home, bringing his wife, but also the shame of a failed enterprise, their love for each other gradually cooled and their reasons for separating increased. The Queen was extremely offended by the King's behavior, saying she had married a monk, not a king."

—*William of Newburgh, Historia Rerum Anglicarum*

In Antioch, Louis and Eleanor were welcomed by Eleanor's uncle, Raymond. Soon, however, a serious rift between Eleanor and Louis became evident. What happened is not exactly clear, and historians, left piecing together the fragmentary evidence, still debate the subject. Louis, with weakened forces (he wrote to Suger on his arrival that most of his barons had died), wanted to continue to Jerusalem in order to finish his intended pilgrimage. But Raymond urged the king to lend his forces toward the siege of Aleppo—the major threat confronting Raymond and also Western hold on the Holy Land. As Louis hesitated, Eleanor began to spend a good deal of time in private talks with her uncle. Eleanor's motivations or aims in these talks are uncertain. She and Raymond may have been discussing possible political actions or Raymond may have been trying to win

Eleanor's help in convincing Louis. Some sources even propose that Eleanor and Raymond became quickly involved in an incestuous romance during the short time she stayed in Antioch.

Whatever the case, Louis objected and decided to set out for Jerusalem. Eleanor refused to go with him. She began to insist that they should have their marriage annulled due to consanguinity. Louis, listening to an advisor, forcibly took Eleanor with him to Antioch. Louis visited holy sites as a pilgrim and participated in a few more mostly unsuccessful military engagements. At last, near Easter of 1149, he resolved it was time to journey back to France.

The remaining company made their way first toward Italy. Louis and Eleanor began the first segment of the journey by sea, where they traveled on different ships. Louis arrived in Italy with no problems, but Eleanor's ship, sailing through a battle between the Normans and the Byzantines, was captured by the Byzantines. However, before long, the Normans seized the ship and delivered Eleanor to Potenza, in southern Italy.

Eleanor and Louis, now reunited, journeyed slowly toward Rome, which they reached in October. There, they met with the Pope. He tried to solve the matter of their marriage by listening to both of them and then declaring that there was no issue with consanguinity—even though previous letters indicate that clergy, including Bernard of Clairvaux, were aware that Eleanor and Louis were closely enough related to have been denied approval for their marriage on this ground. The Pope went so far as to say that anyone who tried to separate Louis and Eleanor again would face excommunication.

Such a declaration could hardly fix the divide that had developed between Louis and Eleanor. Within the following year, Eleanor gave birth to Alix, the couple's second daughter. Still, the division between the two grew until they took action in 1152. By this time, Louis must have agreed with Eleanor that their marriage should end, and in March he produced witnesses to swear to the close kinship between himself and Eleanor. Through this, despite the Pope's earlier warning, he and Eleanor had their marriage legally annulled by the same archbishop who had married them 15 years before.

Now Eleanor was free to act as duchess of Aquitaine in her own right. She immediately rode to her capital of Poitiers to take up this role. Her daughters, the heirs to Aquitaine since Eleanor did not have a son, remained behind with King Louis. In fact, Eleanor's perceived inability to bear a male heir may have been influential in Louis's final decision regarding their divorce, and within two years he married again, this time to Constance of Castile. Louis would soon also forge betrothals for his daughters, Marie and Alix, to build his relationship with his earlier enemy Champagne—an important political move since he had lost control of Aquitaine in divorcing Eleanor.

Eleanor was now also available for marriage, and, with her rich inheritance, she was one of the most eligible women in Europe. In a culture where the use of force was still a potentially accepted route to gaining a wife, Eleanor had to evade abduction on her journey to Poitiers twice—once by Geoffrey of Anjou, brother of Henry Plantagenet, and once by Count Theobald of Blois. However, the two men who tried to marry Eleanor by force were younger sons. As duchess of Aquitaine, she had the potential to make an even better match. That is exactly what she did without delay—within two months of her divorce she would marry again. This time, her husband would be Henry Plantagenet, the duke of the large northern province of Normandy and soon-to-be heir to the throne of England.

Chapter Four

The Queen of England

"She sent secret messengers to the Duke to tell him that she was free again, and urging him to enter into marriage with her. For people said it was she who had cleverly brought about the contrived repudiation."

—Gervase of Canterbury, *Historical Works*

Some writers, including William of Newburgh, suggest that Eleanor had been working to plan her next marriage even before her marriage with Louis was annulled. William further attributes this scheme on Eleanor's part to her desire for a husband whose personality was more like hers and less like "a monk." It is true that Henry could hardly have been compared to an austere and pious monk. He was cultured and well educated, knowledgeable about literature, poetry, and the arts—a mark of the Plantagenet family. He was skilled in riding, hunting, and hawking, and those who described him during his life made note of his seemingly inexhaustible physical energy. Chroniclers called him bold and athletic and mentioned his eloquence as well. Some historians have suggested that Eleanor fell in love with Henry, nine years her junior, during his 1151 visit to the Paris court.

Whether or not love, or at least attraction, formed any part of Eleanor's motivation, it does seem possible and even probable that she did premeditate a marriage to Henry. Several chroniclers besides William of Newburgh also make this claim, and the speed with which the wedding was brought about might indicate prearrangement. On top of this, there were certainly strong political motives for both Eleanor and Henry in achieving a match.

The rumors about Eleanor on the subject of her second marriage do not stop with the idea that it was prearranged. Some sources written 30 to 50 years after that fact claim that she had an affair first with Henry's father, Geoffrey the Fair. Whether there is any truth in these legends, written mainly by authors who took a negative view of Eleanor and the whole Plantagenet family, is difficult to say. These rumors are likely based upon elements of Eleanor's reputation in court and society, and they might also have offered further motivation for Louis in choosing to divorce Eleanor.

Immediately after the divorce, Eleanor sent messages to Henry to let him know her situation. Henry hurried to Poitiers from Lisieux, in Normandy, where he had been in council with his barons. On May 18, 1152, Henry and Eleanor were married in Poitiers in the Cathedral of Saint Pierre. Chroniclers note that the wedding was a smaller and less elaborate event than would have been expected between two persons of Henry and Eleanor's rank. William of Newburgh attributes this to "prudence . . . lest the solemn preparations for such a marriage should case some obstacle to be put in its way." There were several obstacles that very well might have stood in Eleanor and Henry's way, one of which was consanguinity—the very ground which Eleanor and Louis had used to have their marriage annulled. Eleanor and Henry were also closely related.

Additionally, as the duke of Normandy Henry was technically a vassal of the king of France and should have asked Louis for permission to marry according to the customs of the feudal system. Louis would hardly have approved Henry and Eleanor's marriage and seems not to have anticipated it in the slightest. Relations between Henry and Louis had already been tense for some time, with Louis attacking Normandy in 1151. Though a truce had soon been reached through the intercession of Bernard of Clairvaux when Henry and his father came to the French court, he was still a powerful rival and potential threat in Louis's eyes. Henry not only was duke of Normandy but also had come to control other significant areas of France—Anjou and Maine. The alliance with Eleanor brought Aquitaine and Poitou under his sway as well.

Not surprisingly, Eleanor and Henry's marriage quickly brought an end to the peace between Henry and Louis. When Louis heard of the marriage, he regretted divorcing Eleanor and, according to one source, tried to take Henry to court. However, if he did this, it did not work, and Louis soon attacked Normandy along with a number of allies, including Henry's younger brother

Geoffrey of Anjou. A skilled military commander, Henry quickly put down a revolt in Anjou led by Geoffrey.

Leaving the war against Louis's allies still continuing in France, Henry went to England at the beginning of 1153. There, he led his followers in the ongoing civil war against the current king of England, Stephen. Stephen's son, Eustace, was heir to the throne; his death due to sudden illness left Henry in an advantageous position. Henry soon ended the civil war with a truce that made him heir to the English throne upon Stephen's death. After returning from England, Henry soon went to Aquitaine to deal with a revolt there.

Eleanor remained in France while Henry led his armies. What power she had at this time is unclear. Henry's mother, Matilda, held notable sway over Henry, and the charters issued by Eleanor—like most of her actions in Aquitaine when she was the queen of France—are mostly jointly issued with her husband. In August of 1153, Eleanor gave birth to her first child with Henry—a son that was named William. This endangered Louis's situation further, in that he no longer had a future claim to Aquitaine through his daughters; he acknowledged this by giving up the title of duke of Aquitaine.

A little over a year later, on October 25, 1154, King Stephen of England died. Henry and Eleanor prepared to set sail for England, but bad weather delayed the journey for over a month. At last, in December, they arrived. They were crowned as king and queen in Westminster Abbey just a few days before Christmas. Eleanor was not considered very important, as only a few of the chroniclers of the event even mention her presence at the coronation. But it was, nonetheless, the beginning of a new chapter of Eleanor's life as she took on the title of queen of England.

Chapter Five

Continuing Conflict and Courtly Love

"Before the King crossed over [the Channel] on this occasion, the nobles of Maine and Brittany had failed to obey the Queen's orders and, it is said, had sworn to defend one another if they were attacked."

—Robert of Torigni

While Eleanor and Henry's first son, William, died at three years old in 1156, Eleanor proved perfectly capable of bearing more male heirs. Her second son, Henry, was born before William died, in 1155. During the next twelve years, she would have three more sons—Richard, Geoffrey, and John—along with three daughters— Matilda, Eleanor, and Joanna. Despite frequent pregnancies, Eleanor also carried out responsibilities in her roles as queen and duchess. Historians must piece together much of what she did from documents that mention her in passing—the actions of a queen were largely seen as incidental to the activities of male leaders. Yet this does not mean that Eleanor's actions were inconsequential.

Eleanor traveled extensively, frequently crossing the English Channel to appear in England. She also occasionally is recorded appearing with her husband when he held his court in various places. Between mentions of her presence at different times by different chroniclers, historians have drawn an outline of some of Eleanor's journeys and the role she played during her almost 20 years as queen before her relationship with Henry began to deteriorate.

In 1155, Louis and Henry agreed to a temporary peace that would last three years. During 1155, while Henry was away, Eleanor had significant power in England, essentially acting as his regent. She traveled with Henry the following year to Poitou and Aquitaine, by her presence helping him gain recognition of his authority since the territories belonged to her as duchess. After returning to England for a time, she played this role again in late 1158, as Henry dealt with rebels in Poitou. Richard of Poitiers noted Henry's decision to raze the walls of a rebel's castle because he saw "that it would please the queen."

The relationship between Henry and Louis improved significantly as they extended their peace by betrothing Henry and Eleanor's son, young Henry, to Louis's daughter Marguerite. Yet Louis refused to help Henry in his attempt to take Toulouse based on Eleanor's claim to the territory—a project Louis had tried many years before. When Louis arrived within the city, Henry stopped his attack; he did not want to attack Louis, who was his overlord, and break the peace they had obtained. Therefore, the attempt to take Toulouse was a failure.

Soon after, in 1160, Eleanor journeyed back to England to rule for Henry, who was busy with continued fighting on the continent. In this role, Eleanor traveled around England often. She not only issued charters and spent money as she saw fit, but also ruled over England's sheriffs. She returned to Normandy later that year for the wedding of young Henry and Marguerite. Despite their age, the Pope had granted permission for them to marry in return for King Henry's support against the papal rival. This granted Henry possession of the territories that were Marguerite's dowry, and he claimed this possession even before the wedding took place—a move which once again put tension on his relationship with King Louis, leading to continued fighting.

Henry and Eleanor would return to England once again in 1163, just after Henry appointed his close friend and advisor, Thomas Becket, as Archbishop of Canterbury (with the Pope's approval). Much has been made about Eleanor's feelings toward Becket and the idea that she was jealous of his influence over Henry. In fact, this is yet another case of a conjecture that has hardly any grounding in evidence. Soon after he became archbishop, Becket began to support the interests of the church even when these conflicted with the interests of the king, leading to escalating conflict with Henry and eventually to Becket's famous murder. Some scholars come to varied conclusions about Eleanor's role in this conflict, assuming at the least that she must have taken the king's side.

Henry's conflict with Becket exacerbated his conflict with Louis, who not only surprisingly had a son in 1165 with his third wife, Adela of Champagne, but confirmed his alliance with Champagne through the marriages of his and Eleanor's daughters Marie and Alix. Louis, now in a stronger political position, decided to lend his support to Thomas Becket. Eleanor and Matilda did arrange for the count of Flanders to work for reconciliation. Becket hoped Eleanor might support him, but the one mention of Eleanor in relation to these events is a letter from a clergyman to Becket that says Eleanor could not be expected to assist him due to the influence of Raoul de Faye, her uncle.

Eleanor would go with Henry to England again in 1166, only to have Henry leave and then quickly return. The reason for his hasty return was unusual—the nobles refused to obey the queen's orders in the king's absence. Henry quickly quashed the brewing rebellion, using it to place the region of Brittany more firmly under his control. With this exception, it seems that Eleanor's periods of ruling in England in place of her husband were generally politically successful.

It was probably within a year of this time, around when Eleanor gave birth to her last child, John, that some scholars speculate she discovered Henry's affair with his mistress Rosamond Clifford. According to some sources, Henry had openly moved Rosamond into one of his palaces near Oxford. Other scholars conjecture that Eleanor probably already knew about the king's infidelity—of which this was hardly the first instance—

but it was the openness of this affair that angered the queen. Though some scholars impute Eleanor's actions during the following decade to a desire for revenge, in reality, her motives are as uncertain as in much of her life.

Eleanor and Henry continued in similar patterns for the next few years, with Eleanor filling in for Henry in England periodically until about 1168, when she seems to have remained at Poitiers, and Henry putting down revolts—which were more or less openly instigated by Louis—in Aquitaine.

These are also the years that, according to legend, Eleanor held "courts of love" at Poitiers, where she and her daughter Marie ruled on questions of love based on the ideas of courtly love promoted by Eleanor's troubadour grandfather—an event that supposedly contributed to the spread of the ideals of courtly love in literature, music, and art. While Eleanor may well have had an impact on the spread of the concept of courtly love, the "courts of love" are almost certainly a myth and even Eleanor's influence on the arts is highly debated. What is clear, on the other hand, is that by this point, Eleanor's own marriage with King Henry was in drastic decline; the two seem to have rarely been even at the same place at the same time. The next decade would reveal the extreme extent of the tension between England's king and queen.

Chapter Six

At the Center of Rebellion

"The instigators of that direful treachery were Louis, King of France, and even—so some people said—Eleanor, Queen of England, and Raoul de Faye. For at that time the Queen had in her charge her sons Richard, Duke of Aquitaine, and Geoffrey, Count of Brittany, and she sent them to their brother the Young King in France, to stand together with his against the King their father."

—Roger of Howden, *Chronica*

By 1170, King Henry had become seriously ill. He decided the time had come to crown his oldest son, Henry, to make sure that the throne passed smoothly from father to son. Thomas Becket refused to support this move and even worked against it. Consequently, the king, in England, and Eleanor, in Normandy, commanded all the ports that linked England and the continent to be closed. This would prevent the arrival of an order from the church that could affect the coronation. According to one source, Eleanor was in full support and even encouraged young Henry's early coronation. This would make sense, as it would give more power to one of her sons rather than King Henry and seems to be confirmed by records of her orders to stop ships from traveling to England.

By September of 1170, the ailing King Henry had become so ill that he appears to have thought his death was imminent. He divided his lands to his four sons. His second son, Richard, would inherit Eleanor's lands in Aquitaine—an arrangement that Eleanor had already been working towards. She traveled through her holdings with Richard at her side several times, an act that affirmed his future power there. Though Henry did not die in 1170, he remained quite ill. During the following year, Richard went through the ceremonies that made him count of Poitou and duke of Aquitaine. Around the same time, Henry and Eleanor's third son, Geoffrey, was taking up power in Brittany.

Unexpectedly, King Henry recovered. As his health revived, he had no intention of passing on independent power to his sons. In his eyes, their investiture in their inherited lands was ceremonial, intended to make the king's intentions clear. Not surprisingly, Henry's three teenaged sons (John was still a young child) took a different view of the matter, and Eleanor supported her sons. King Louis may also have been influential in counseling his son-in-law, young Henry, to demand more independence. King Henry's expectation of maintaining his dominance became increasingly evident as he made choices such as taking castles from young Henry's holdings to use as part of the marriage contract the king was arranging for John. The attitude among the three princes soon began to turn resentful, but King Henry either did not care or was oblivious.

Soon a conspiracy was in the works, involving young Henry, Richard, Geoffrey, Eleanor, and possibly King Louis. Though King Henry was tipped off to the potential of revolt, it seems he did not take this information very seriously. He began to watch young Henry more carefully, but not Eleanor or their other sons.

In March of 1173, the growing unrest exploded in action as young Henry absconded to the French court of King Louis. Louis began to make it clear that he would support young Henry, rather than King Henry II, as the current and rightful king of England. He found allies for the prince and refused to turn him back to his father. King Henry now realized that young Henry was actively rebelling, and the king turned to strengthening his military defenses. But it seems he still did not anticipate the extent of the revolt that he had on his hands—that Eleanor would incite Richard and Geoffrey to throw their weight behind the rebellion. This involvement on Eleanor's part is well established; the queen is attributed with more or less blame for the rebellion of her sons—and particularly the participation of Richard and Geoffrey—in numerous sources.

In Paris, King Louis knighted 16-year-old Richard, a ceremony that recognized him as a man able to hold the role of a warrior, defender of his territory, and independent ruler—a very political move that essentially acknowledged Richard as the current rightful ruler of Aquitaine. The three brothers and King Louis soon continued the rebellion with an offensive in Normandy, conducted with the aid of their allies, the king of Scotland

and the counts of Boulogne, Flanders, and Blois. King Henry was quick to respond, hiring mass numbers of mercenaries, whose loyalty could be counted on as long as they were paid. He met with his sons and King Louis to discuss terms of peace, offering a few concessions to his sons but still unwilling to turn over much real power. Young Henry, Richard, and Geoffrey refused his terms, and the war carried on with the brothers attempting a failed attack across the Channel in England.

As the rebellion progressed, it became ever more obvious to King Henry and to other leaders of the day that Eleanor was highly involved. The archbishop of Rouen wrote to her, trying to coerce her to return to her husband and resume the acceptable Christian behavior of a wife within marriage. He warned that setting herself against her husband would "cause general ruin" and "bring harm to all," and informed Eleanor that she alone would be to blame for the results of her "foolish decisions." While these charges likely sound extreme to modern readers, they aptly show the thought of the day in regards to a woman's position as a wife.

But no matter what the church and the norms of her society urged, Eleanor had no intention of giving up the revolt and being reconciled to Henry. She took further action, raising Aquitaine and Poitou to join the rebellion. In November, Henry arrived in southern France to quell the rebels. He steadily took territory, approaching the lands held by Eleanor's uncle Raoul de Faye, where Eleanor was staying. Eleanor, realizing she would soon be surrounded, attempted an escape. According to Gervase of Canterbury, she fled in disguise as a man—yet another disreputable choice from a medieval perspective. She hoped to reunite with her sons, but despite her disguise, Eleanor was captured on her way to Chartres and held as a prisoner at Chinon. While this did not end the revolt, it did end Eleanor's role in it.

Chapter Seven

Fifteen Years of Captivity

"It was at that period that the meaning of the prophecy came to light, concealed as it had been until then by the obscurity of its wording: 'The eagle of the broken alliance will rejoice in its third brood.' The eagle must refer to the Queen, because she spread her wings over two kingdoms . . . Richard, her third son, denoted by the phrase 'the third brood,' strove in all things to exalt his mother's name."

—Ralph of Diceto, *Historical Works*

As the rebellion continued without Eleanor, King Henry soon defeated Richard in Aquitaine, leaving Richard and his few remaining men to retreat to the castle of Taillebourg. Henry then turned his attention toward Brittany and Normandy. At last, heading back to England to deal with the rebellion there, he took Eleanor with him as a captive. She had—not surprisingly—entirely lost his trust, and to avoid any further revolts, Henry placed her under house arrest in Salisbury. For Eleanor, this was the beginning of a long 15 years of captivity.

King Henry quashed the rebellion in England quickly, soon capturing the king of Scotland. From there, he returned to Normandy, where he defeated King Louis at Rouen. As the situation became more hopeless for the rebels, Louis and young Henry finally made a truce with the English king. Richard, however, tried to hold out, continuing to fight in Poitou. At last, as King Henry arrived in the south to face Richard, he too realized that it was time to give up the fight. At long last, in September of 1174, Henry and his three sons reached an agreed-upon peace. The three princes had to settle for less control than they had wanted over their territories and had to swear never to rebel against Henry again. Many of the other rebels were pardoned, and Richard would now return to Aquitaine to work for peace on Henry's behalf.

The revolt that Eleanor had contributed to and perhaps even instigated had failed dramatically, and she herself was hated by the king and now a prisoner. Though she appears to have moved around in England at times, she was under constant surveillance and was not at liberty. Additionally, King Henry was seriously considering divorce, which he might have achieved on the same grounds of consanguinity that Louis and Eleanor had used for their divorce. By now, Eleanor was 51 years old, and so this threat was more significant to her than her divorce from Louis had been.

But Henry's plans for divorce were halted by the papal representative, who seems to have realized Henry's actual goal: freedom to marry Rosamond, his mistress. This was hardly an end approved of by the church. In addition to this, it was not long before Rosamond became ill and died in 1176. Legends that tell of Eleanor playing a role in Rosamond's death sprung up after the fact, but they have no basis on evidence.

Even at the time of Eleanor's captivity, she had become associated with a well-known prophecy supposed spoken by Merlin and circulated through Geoffrey of Monmouth's *The History of the Kings of Britain*. The prophecy spoke of an eagle with two heads, and this picture came to be associated with the strong figure of Eleanor even in her lifetime. King Henry is recorded as seeing himself and his sons in other aspects of the prophecy, though he was confused by it because he and his sons seemed to have achieved peace and Eleanor was safely out of the way.

Though Eleanor was no longer involved in any plots against Henry, her three sons were not as obedient as they had acted under duress, and conflict would soon break out again. First, when Richard faced trouble subduing his vassals in Aquitaine (according to the barons this was because of his overly brutal methods), King Henry went to help him and called for his other sons to join him. However, young Henry, the heir who still had no actual power while Richard had at least some, decided to join the Aquitanian rebels instead. It seems that the king, trying to assuage the rivalry between the two brothers, ordered Richard and the younger Geoffrey to pay homage to their brother Henry. Richard, in his turn, refused to do this, arguing that he owed submission only to his father and that, after all, Aquitaine was his inheritance from his mother so it was not subject to Henry anyway. War broke out again.

Now Richard and King Henry were pitched against young Henry, who was supported by the new king of

France, Louis's son Philip Augustus, as well as Geoffrey. Before long, young Henry and his rebel followers ran out of money, even plundering churches to raise the funds they needed to continue the fight. Then, young Henry became ill in the early summer of 1183. He sent a message to his father, informing him that he expected to die and wanted to be reconciled first. Unfortunately, he had sent messages like this previously as ploys, and King Henry did not believe him this time when he was telling the truth. In June, Henry died. One of his last requests was for his father to treat Eleanor more kindly. According to one chronicler, before she heard the news of young Henry's death, Eleanor had a dream where she saw her deceased son wearing a heavenly crown.

The revolt was ended with young Henry's death, and Geoffrey was punished with the loss of territory. Yet the family's troubles were not over, and Eleanor was soon to become minimally involved again—this time in the interest of peace. Richard had become heir to England, and King Henry wished to rearrange the distribution of other territories, giving Aquitaine to his favorite and youngest son, John. Richard flatly refused the idea of giving up Aquitaine. Not long after, John joined Geoffrey on an offensive against Richard.

Perhaps in an attempt to reconcile his sons, and also in a political move aimed to avoid returning Marguerite's dower to the king of France, King Henry now offered Eleanor limited freedom—a respite from her captivity of almost 12 years. She is mentioned as going to speak to her daughter Matilda, at that time duchess of Saxony, and

Henry even gave his wife gifts. During the latter half of 1184, Henry called his sons to England, and they eventually formed a peace treaty; Eleanor, who was present at court at the time, was probably involved in this process.

But this peace, like so many attempts before, would not last. It was only months later that the brothers began to fight again. King Henry once more tried using Eleanor to bring peace. This time he took her to Normandy and returned her territories of Aquitaine and Poitou to her. Richard could not very well fight against his mother, as her favorite son and her heir, so he submitted to this return of Eleanor as duchess of Aquitaine. While she held some power again, King Henry held most of it. After this, Eleanor's name fades to the background of the records once again, so it is probable that she returned to a state of captivity.

Suddenly and unexpectedly, in 1186, Geoffrey died—possibly from an accident in a tournament. He had been about to perform homage to the king of France, Philip Augustus, and his death made a war between France on one side and King Henry and his remaining sons on the other look inevitable. Yet Richard managed to develop a truce; in his position as intermediary, he became close friends with Philip Augustus and went to Paris. There, he heard rumors of his father's intentions to change his inheritance again, giving the major province of Anjou, and maybe Poitou as well, to John.

The father and son met Philip Augustus to discuss peace in late 1188. However, negotiations went downhill quickly, and the talks ended with Richard doing homage to Philip, not Henry. Another attempt at peace the following year was likewise unsuccessful. Richard and Philip chased King Henry to Tours, in Normandy. Finally, Henry had come to the end of his resources. Even his son John had joined the rebellion against him. Soon after, in July of 1189, King Henry—grieved, tired, and ill—died at nearby Chinon.

Upon Henry's death, Richard became the king of England. His first move was to fulfill Merlin's prophecy by ordering the release of his mother, the "eagle." Eleanor was already free by the time Richard's representative arrived, and Richard gave her power over England. She immediately set free others who, like herself, had been imprisoned for political reasons. Eleanor, having outlived both her royal husbands, had risen to become queen once again.

Chapter Eight

Queen Mother

"[Richard] kept with him the maiden he loved and sent his mother to take care of the country he had left behind, so that his honour would be safe. Appointed to share with her the task of ruling England was Walter, Archbishop of Rouen, a very sensible man; he had plenty of fighting to do."

—Ambroise, L'Estoire de la Guerre Sainte

Richard, often known as Richard the Lionheart, was crowned in September of 1189, with Eleanor present at the coronation. Soon, however, Richard had vowed to set off on the Third Crusade. Richard left the government of England in the hands of a few selected men, a Council of Regency. However, he also provided Eleanor, as the queen mother, with a significantly increased income, allowing her great freedom to independently exercise the power she held over England's barons.

After numerous delays, Richard finally left for the Holy Land in 1190. On his way, in Cyprus, Richard married Berengaria of Navarre. Eleanor was involved with negotiating the marriage agreement. Historians used to believe that Eleanor coordinated the match without Richard's approval and forced him into it, but the more current view is that the two worked together—a coordination perhaps necessary to success, since Richard had, in fact, already been long betrothed to Philip Augustus's half-sister Alys. Eleanor traveled to Italy to bring Berengaria where Richard currently was staying in Sicily. The journey was probably not an easy one, as it involved crossing the Alps in winter.

Eleanor only stayed with Richard a few days, soon leaving him with his new wife and his sister Joanna to continue on with the crusade. Eleanor, for her part, traveled first to Rome, where she succeeded in having the Pope appoint the deceased Henry's increasingly powerful bastard son as an archbishop, thereby preventing him from seizing political power while Richard was gone. At last, she returned to Normandy.

From 1191 until Richard's eventual return, Eleanor played a significant role in England. Governance of England turned out to be a difficult task, as the men who held power were soon in conflict, and John was busy scheming to take power for himself. Additionally, there was a threat to the Plantagenet holdings on the continent from Philip Augustus, who returned early from the crusade. Eleanor did her best to maintain order on Richard's behalf. But the threat from Philip only increased as it became apparent that he and John might be conspiring together. She managed to prevent John from traveling to meet with Philip, but she also wrote to Richard and warned him that if he did not return home quickly, he might lose his country.

Richard listened. In September of 1192, he made a treaty with his enemy Saladin and started for home. But on the way home, he was captured by his European enemies and held captive until 1194. This gave John an opening to join Philip and take power; Eleanor was unable to keep him in check this time. When the two intended to invade England, Eleanor anticipated them, preparing defenses that caused them to stop the attempt. John went back to England, where he caused trouble by spreading rumors of Richard's death and trying to spark a rebellion. Eleanor and the Council of Regency, along with loyal barons, took back the castles that John captured.

Eleanor's primary occupation, however, was the negotiation of a ransom to redeem Richard from captivity. When she succeeded in these negotiations, she took charge of the collection of the ransom—a colossal sum. When she had most of the ransom, she traveled to Germany to redeem Richard. There, she turned over the money she had as well as hostages, including two of her grandsons. Finally, in February of 1194, Richard was freed to return to England. He traveled through his holding on the continent, making his power more secure. At last, arriving in England, he dealt with the rebels. He also soon participated in a second coronation, at which Eleanor took a seat of honor and Richard's wife, Berengaria, was not even present.

When Richard left England again not long afterward, he did not know that he would never return. He reconciled with John, quite possibly due to Eleanor's influence. In the next few years, Richard seemed to be increasing in his success as a ruler. But in 1199, putting down another small revolt in the ever-unruly Aquitaine, Richard received a wound from a crossbow bolt which became infected. He sent for Eleanor, who arrived in time to be with him when he died.

The drama of Eleanor's life did not end with Richard's death. During John's coronation, Eleanor was involved with leading a war on the continent—defending John's right to the throne from her 12-year-old grandson, Arthur, who was backed by Philip. Though in her 70s, she still seemed to have ceaseless energy. She issued orders, created charters, maneuvered politically with the church and with other rulers, and, in general, acted as queen to achieve peace.

When John and Philip arranged for Philip's heir Louis to marry one of John's nieces, the aging Eleanor went to Spain to choose between the two nieces. On the way, she was ambushed and captured by Hugh le Brun—a vassal who refused to recognize Plantagenet rule—and had to negotiate her freedom. After going to Castile, she returned to Normandy.

When war broke out once more between England and France, Eleanor stepped into the middle of things. Traveling toward Poitiers, she took refuge in the city of Mirabeau just as Arthur's forces besieged it. According to one source, she refused to give up the city in exchange for being allowed to leave. Instead she managed to get a message to John, who came with great haste and rescued her, also capturing Arthur. The war continued, but Eleanor did not live to see much more of it.

In April 1204, she died, perhaps at Poitiers or, as most historians now think, at Fontevraud Abbey, near Chinon, where she had frequently resided during her life. She was buried at Fontevraud alongside her second husband Henry and—perhaps more importantly to Eleanor—her son Richard the Lionheart.

Conclusion

It is difficult to make judgments about Eleanor's character based on the often-fragmentary pieces of information available about her life. Were her choices wise? How accurate are the medieval sources that speak of her, many of which take a negative view of this powerful and unusual woman? Certainly, she was not afraid to assert herself, as she did when she tried to refuse to go on to Jerusalem with her first husband, King Louis. She also took bold action despite the council of those around her, as she did when she incited her sons to rebellion. She survived through adversity, waiting for a chance for change through 15 long years of being a prisoner under her husband Henry. And she exercised great political power, especially as her life went on and her son Richard became king.

In light of these feats that paint Eleanor as one of the middle ages' most bold and dynamic characters, it is easy to forget that she was also a real person. She endured failed marriages, arranged uncertain political marriages for her children, watched her sons fight each other and all but one die before her, and struggled to bring her most beloved son back home. What she thought or felt about most of the events of her life, what she enjoyed, what motivated her—to all of these questions we can only conjecture answers. It is no surprise that Eleanor of Aquitaine's life has become shrouded in legends. An unforgettable character like hers is the material of legends—an invitation to try to imagine the lost details of the story that we will never know in full.

Manufactured by Amazon.ca
Bolton, ON

33176548R10028